Object Talks

on the Teachings of Jesus

STANDARD PUBLISHING

Cincinnati, Ohio   2858

Illustrated by Richard Briggs

ISBN: 0-87239-722-X

Scripture Text: The Holy Bible, New International Version. Copyright © 1978 by New York International Bible Society. Used by permission of New York International Bible Society.

Contents

Identify This

Every good tree bears good fruit, but a bad tree bears bad fruit . . . Thus, by their fruit you will recognize them. —*Matthew 7:17, 20*

Objects Needed: A variety of bare branches

These branches were cut from some trees in my yard. Can you tell what kind of trees the branches came from? They seem much the same. They are all brownish-green. They have no leaves.

If this branch had leaves or blossoms on it perhaps you would be able to identify it as a branch from an apple tree. The other branches were taken from a plum tree and a cherry tree. It is difficult to know the difference.

If you could look at these branches in the summer when they are producing fruit you would be able to easily identify the tree. When you see juicy cherries hanging from the branches you know exactly what kind of tree it is. The same would be true with apple trees, plum trees, orange trees, and lemon trees.

The Bible tells us that, "by their fruit you will recognize them," and that is certainly true.

The Bible also tells us that when the Holy Spirit controls our lives, He will produce fruit in us. Can you think of some kinds of fruit that people produce? The fruit of the Spirit are love, joy, peace, patience, kindness, goodness, faithfulness, gentleness, and self-control.

Christians can be identified by the fruit they produce just as you could identify a tree by the fruit that grows on it.

We should try to let God control our lives so that we can be like the fruit tree and produce fruit that others can enjoy.

—*Lois Edstrom*

Ask, Seek, and Knock

Ask and it will be given to you; seek and you will find; knock and the door will be opened to you. —*Matthew 7:7*

Object Needed: A large calendar, showing one month

Here is a calendar of a whole month. When we look at it we might see it as thirty days. Or we might see it as four weeks and two days. Or we might see it as thirty new and wonderful opportunities to serve God and to help our prayers to be answered. How can we help to make our prayers answered? Let me tell you about it—it's really very simple.

Suppose you want a new bicycle very much. Each night you pray that when you wake up, a new bicycle will be parked by your front door. Each morning when you awaken you run to the front door, but there is no bicycle standing there waiting for you. You could pray that same prayer for a bicycle every day this month—in fact you could pray that same prayer every day for a whole year—but still no red bicycle would be parked at your front door in answer to your prayers.

But every day God will send us ways to make ourselves useful to others at home and in the neighborhood. God sends us opportunities to show that we deserve such a gift and that we are trying to do our part in helping ourselves get that new bike.

Jesus taught us to "Ask, seek, and knock" (Matthew 7:7). To *ask* means using our lips to pray. That means asking with a sincere heart. *Seek* means keeping our eyes open so we see the opportunities God sends to us as answers to our prayers. *Knock* means using our hands, our feet, our minds, our abilities, energy, courage, wisdom and strength to do our best to make the most of the opportunities God sends to us each day.

And the door will be opened to you. If we pray believing, if we keep our eyes open to the blessings God sends us, if we try earnestly to do our best in every way each day, God promises to hear our prayers and send us even more than we ever dreamed of asking for.

—*Idalee Vonk*

Be Free

So if the Son sets you free, you will be free indeed. —*John 8:36*

Object Needed: A picture of a spider or web

Have you ever gone outside on an autumn morning to look for spider webs? When you find one, take time to enjoy its beauty and study how wondrously it is constructed. Perhaps you will be able to watch a spider in the process of building a web.

At the back portion of a spider are two to four pairs of silk glands, called spinnerets, that contain many spinning tubes. Out of these tubes ooze a thick, sticky fluid that hardens into silken threads. These spinning tubes move like fingers and can twist, pull, or weave the fluid into the right kind of thread. Different types of lines are used for various purposes. One kind of thread may be used to attach the web to a leaf while a different line is needed for the spider to dangle from a branch. Another type of thread will be spun to send or receive messages.

To construct a web the spider first builds a frame with strong supporting threads. After establishing a hub in the center, the spider spins a series of spokes to the outside.

Then, lines are added in a circular pattern until a beautiful and useful web is completed.

The web is used to trap insects for food. When an insect hits the web and struggles, the vibrations signal the spider. The spider rushes to the trapped insect, wraps it in a band of silk threads until the insect is completely helpless. When an insect becomes *entangled* in a spider web it is unable to escape.

Have you ever said something that wasn't true? When that happens the feeling can be similar to what happens to an insect in a spider web. As we struggle to keep our friends and family from knowing the truth, we become *entangled* in our problem until we feel helpless. We get caught and wrapped up in a web of lies and we think there is no escape.

Unlike the insect trapped in the web, we can choose to be free. The Bible assures us of freedom in John 8:36. "So if the Son sets you free, you will be free indeed."

If we trust in the power of Jesus Christ we will have freedom to be the best person that we can be. We will be able to live a truthful life and be free from the tangle of mistakes we have made in the past.

Don't get trapped in a web of untruthfulness. Choose freedom through Jesus Christ.

—*Lois Edstrom*

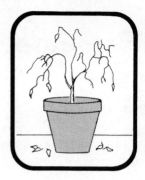

Help Your Faith to Grow

I am the light of the world. Whoever follows me will never walk in darkness, but will have the light of life. —*John 8:12*

Object Needed: A dried up or wilted plant that has been left in the dark

Can anyone tell me what would happen if I put an artificial plant in the dark and kept it there for a long time? Nothing, right? An artificial plant does not need any sunshine. It would continue to look just the same, except perhaps for the dust that might collect on it.

But what would happen to a real plant if you left it in the dark for several weeks? It would wither up and die and look like this plant I have here (show the plant to the children). It is possible, if I were to do just the right things, for this plant to grow again because it comes from a bulb. But if it is left in the dark it will never grow again.

As Christians, it is important for us not to keep our faith hidden from others. If we do, it will never really grow. Jesus wants us to let other people know about Him so that He can help them, *and* so that our own faith will grow.

So if we really want our faith to grow, we must be willing to speak up about our faith and follow Jesus' teachings even if that is not always very popular. Sometimes others may make fun of us for being Christians and believing what we do and living the way Jesus wants us to. But if we don't, our faith may end up like this plant that was kept hidden away in the dark—all dried up, withered away, and of no use to anyone or anything.

—*Duane Kellogg*

Advertisements for Jesus

All men will know that you are my disciples if you love one another.   —*John 13:35*

Objects Needed: Some magazine ads that have pictures of smiling people

If you had something that you wanted to sell, one of the first things you would have to do is let other people know about it. That's called advertising. We see lots of advertisements on TV or in magazines. Have you ever noticed how the people in advertisements always look happy?

I brought some examples along this morning that I got out of a magazine. See how happy these people look? (Show them the ads and ask what products are being sold.) Do you know why they usually use happy looking people in advertisements? So that when people see pictures like these, they will want to buy the products, because they hope they will be as happy as the people in the ads. What would happen if they used sad or angry looking people instead? (People wouldn't want to buy the product.)

In a way, as Christians, we are like advertisements for Jesus. If people know that we are Christians, and if they like what they see when they look at us, maybe they will want to know Jesus too. But it works the other way also. If people see us grumbling or fighting or complaining all the time, they probably won't want to know more about Jesus. At least they won't want to hear about Him from us.

Jesus came to bring us joy and peace. He came to make our lives complete. He tells us that if we do the things He says, then we will be filled with His joy. So if you want to be a good advertisement for Jesus, remember to follow His commandments. Then He will fill you with joy, so that when other people look at you they will want what you have—the joy of Jesus.   —*Duane Kellogg*

10

Tell Others About Jesus

Go and make disciples of all nations, baptizing them in the name of the Father and of the Son and of the Holy Spirit, and teaching them to obey everything I have commanded you.
—*Matthew 28:19, 20*

Objects Needed: Two candles

In a way, this candle shows what we are like before we become Christians (show one unlit candle). All our parts are there—we have bodies, minds, and spirits—but something is missing. We lack the light and the warmth that only God can give us. But when we accept Jesus as our Savior and Lord, His love lights up our lives and we shine for Him (light the candle).

Once we become Christians we will want to share this warmth and light with others. We can do this at home and at school and everywhere we go. We can tell others about Jesus, we can be friends with someone that no one else likes, we can help our parents at home and do what they tell us. When we do these things, we share God's love with others (light the other candle with the one already lit), and they in turn will want to shine for Him as well.

Notice that even though this candle was used to light the other, the flame is still the same size as it was before. The same holds true when we share God's love with others. God never takes any of His love away from us. So remember to be good witnesses for Jesus Christ. Share what you know and have experienced of Him with others.

—*Duane Kellogg*

11

The Right Touch

People brought all their sick to him and begged him to let the sick just touch the edge of his cloak, and all who touched him were healed. —*Matthew 14:36*

Objects Needed: Sandpaper; a block of wood

Do you know what this is? Sandpaper. Notice how scratchy and rough it is?

Have you ever watched anyone use sandpaper? Let's all take a turn rubbing a piece of wood with the sandpaper and see what happens. The gritty paper removes the *rough spots* from the wood and makes it *smooth.* The more the sandpaper is rubbed against the wood, the smoother the wood becomes.

Have you ever had a "bad day?" Everything seemed to go wrong. Your brother hollered at you. You forgot to make your bed and your mother had to remind you. It rained and you couldn't play outside. Your sister ate all the cookies! We can all think of things that irritate us and make us feel rough and angry.

We can use those rough spots in our lives to become better people. If we ask for God's love, He will touch us and smooth away our anger in much the same way the sandpaper smoothes wood. We can experience His forgiveness and replace our irritations with a feeling of care and concern for others. When we feel God's love, we can then touch others with that love.

The more we ask for and receive God's touch, the better we will feel. Let Him smooth away your rough spots and polish your life to a fine shine.

—*Lois Edstrom*

Follow Me

I am the way and the truth and the life. No one comes to the Father except through me.
—John 14:6

Object Needed: Picture of a German Shepherd guide dog; or perhaps the testimony of a blind person from your church or community. If the situation permits, blindfold some of the children and ask them to perform a few simple tasks under your supervision.

Have you ever been lost? You probably felt frightened and alone. You didn't know which way to go. Nothing seemed familiar.

Some people have lost their sight and had to learn how to move around in the world even though they are surrounded by darkness. People who are blind have probably experienced some of the same sensations you felt when you were lost.

Here are pictures of some wonderful dogs who are training to be guide dogs for the blind. These dogs must have a special personality. They are chosen while they are still puppies to do very important work.

It is a beautiful sight to see a guide dog in a harness leading his master on shopping trips, to work, or to school.

A blind person must learn to trust the guide dog and be willing to work together with the dog as a team. The dog could not do its job properly if the master continually jerked on the harness or was afraid to let the dog lead. A sightless person must believe that his animal can do the job for which it is trained and have the courage to follow.

The same principle applies to our relationship with God. Jesus said, "No one comes to the Father except through me." We must have the courage to ask for help and be willing to work together with others to find the Way, which is Jesus Christ. Then, we must trust Him to care for us and help us discover what is right for us. If we hesitate or try to do things our own way we hinder His leading. Just as a blind person must keep his hand on the harness and move confidently along, so must we keep our hands on God's Word. Even though we can't see what is ahead, we must have faith that together we will reach our destination.

Because of the love and trust that grows between the guide dog and its master, they become lifelong friends.

By having faith and following Jesus Christ, you will also find a lifelong friend.

—*Lois Edstrom*

Fair Play

In everything do to others what you would have them do to you.   —*Matthew 7:12*

Objects Needed: A checkerboard and checkers

Here we have a checkerboard with the checkers arranged on it, ready to start a game. We can't just place the checkers wherever we please, because there are rules that tell us the right way to arrange the checkers on the board. These rules also tell us the right way to play the game. Everyone who wants to play checkers must learn these rules. Then, after he knows the rules, he must play the game according to them.

Let's suppose you and I are playing a game of checkers. We both know the rules, but I don't want to follow them. First of all, I arrange the checkers on the board, not according to the rules, but the way I want to. You, of course, want to arrange the checkers the right way, according to the rules. So at the very beginning of our game, I would be starting trouble.

Then all the while we played, let's suppose I want everything done my way—not according to the rules, but according to my own ideas. When it's my turn I move twice instead of just once, so I will have twice as many turns as you. I move my checkers all over the board, but I want you to move yours only in one direction. I will not remove my checkers from the board when you jump them with your checkers, but I say you must remove all your checkers that I jump with mine.

How long do you suppose you would want to play with me? Not very long, because I am not playing fairly. In many ways I would be cheating. I wouldn't be giving you a fair chance to win.

In every game there are certain rules that tell us the right way to play. If we don't follow the rules, we are not playing the game fairly.

When we cheat while playing a game, we are really cheating ourselves more than we are cheating the other players, for in the end we hurt ourselves more than we hurt them. No one will want to play with us, and soon we'll find we don't have any friends. In that way we would be cheating ourselves more than anyone else. And on top of all that, there is no way we can keep God from knowing that we have cheated.

—Idalee Vonk

How Much Can God Give?

Jesus said to them, "Only in his home town . . . is a prophet without honor." He could not do any miracles there. . . . And he was amazed at their lack of faith. —Mark 6:4-6

Objects Needed: A jar filled with water and a large rock

As you can all see, I brought a jar filled with water with me this morning. Even though I would like to, I couldn't put much more water in this jar without having it spill all over, could I? It's holding just about all the water it can.

Well, no, not really. What do you think will happen if I remove the rock that is in the jar? Let's take it out and see (remove rock). Wow, now look at all the room there is to add more water! That rock was making it so I could add very little more water, but without it, I can add a whole lot more.

Did you know that the same kind of thing can happen in our lives? As I am sure you all know, God has lots of good things He would like to put into our lives—like I wanted to put more water in this jar—but because of our disbelief, or lack of interest, or unthankfulness, which are like big rocks in us, God cannot add any more good things to our lives.

Until we get rid of these bad things, we won't be able to receive the good things that God wants to give us, simply because we have no room. We need to take a look at ourselves to see if we have things in our lives that prevent God from giving us more. If we do, then we need to ask God to help us get rid of them. He's just waiting to fill up our lives with every good thing that we need.

—Duane Kellogg

Seeking Jesus

For everyone who asks receives; he who seeks finds; and to him who knocks, the door will be opened. — *Matthew 7:8*

Object Needed: A shoebox with a picture of Jesus inside

I need a volunteer to help me this morning. Does anybody want to give me a hand? (Do this near a place where a child can get up on something and easily look in the box.) Inside this shoebox I have a picture of a very important person. I want you to take a look inside so you can see who it is. (Hold the box just high enough so the child cannot see from the floor, but could see by climbing up on something.)

Can you tell me who it is? Oh, you can't see—I guess because you are not tall enough. Do you think if you tried real hard you could think of a way to see whose picture is in this box? You could climb up on something and look in, couldn't you? Go ahead and take a look. It's a picture of Jesus, isn't it? Thank you for your help. You may sit down.

Jesus came into this world in order to seek and to save people like you and me. But we can't expect Him to do everything. He expects us to at least meet Him part way by putting in some effort to seek Him, like _____ (volunteer's name) had to do to see this picture of Jesus. One way we can do that is by going where we know we will be able to see Him. And where might that be? (Let them guess.) That's right—church, Sunday school, vacation Bible school, Bible club, youth groups, and so forth. We also can see Him by reading the Bible. It takes some effort on our part to do these things. Sometimes we would rather stay in bed, or watch TV, or go out and play.

But if we really want to get to see and know Jesus ourselves, then we have to do something about it. And when

17

we do, Jesus will reward our efforts by coming into our lives and hearts in a most wonderful way.

—Duane Kellogg

Forgive Each Other

If your brother sins, rebuke him, and if he repents, forgive him.   —Luke 17:3

Object Needed: A knife

Who would like to volunteer this morning to help me? (Choose a volunteer.) Okay, I want you to tell me which part of your body I may cut off with this knife (pull out a sharp knife). How about a finger, a toe, an arm, an ear? No? Why not? Would you say you *need* all those parts?

The Bible says that the church is like a body. Every member of a church is important to the rest of the members, because we all depend on each other like parts of a physical body.

But sometimes we cut members off that body by not forgiving them when they do something we don't like. When we do this, then we are hurting ourselves—just as if we cut one of our fingers off.

Jesus tells us that we *must* forgive one another because this is our duty as Christians. This is what He expects of us because He has forgiven *us* so many times.

Try to remember this the next time someone does something against you. Ask God to help you forgive those who hurt you or treat you unfairly.

—Duane Kellogg

Growing Strong in the Lord

And Jesus grew in wisdom and stature, and in favor with God and men. —*Luke 2:52*

Objects Needed: Some acorns and a small branch of an oak tree

One of the most beautiful trees in any season is the sturdy oak. We can see by the leaves that the tree from which we clipped this branch is an oak tree. Have you ever thought, when you looked at a large oak with widespreading branches and a thick trunk, that it grew out of a tiny acorn? But the acorn had to be a good acorn. An acorn that is wormy or rotten inside is of no use to anyone.

Just as strong oak trees are grown from good acorns, so strong men and women grow from good habits. Good habits are just as important to our growth as good acorns are to the growth of an oak tree.

An oak tree that has grown strong can stand firmly against the hardest winter winds. And during the summer its spreading branches can provide pleasant shade over a wide area around it. A man or woman who has grown strong because of good habits can stand firmly against wickedness, temptations, and troubles. They will be able to be a good example to others, just as the oak gives coolness and shade to all who stand in the shade of its branches.

But the oak tree didn't grow from a tiny acorn to a huge tree overnight; it took many years. That's the way with our lives. We don't grow up overnight. It takes years of loving God and trying to follow His Word for us to grow into useful, helpful Christian men and women. So it's very important that we begin now—today—to do only those things, think only those things, and say only those things that will help us to grow strong in the Lord.

—*Idalee Vonk*

Loyalty to Friends

Greater love has no one than this, that one lay down his life for his friends.

—John 15:13

Objects Needed: Two bowls of water; two pieces of cloth, one dyed with fast colors and one dyed with color that runs (if no material can be found with color that runs, dye a piece of white cloth using vegetable coloring in cold water)

These two pieces of material are alike in many ways. They are both made of cotton. The weave is the same. That tells us they were both woven on the same kind of loom. They are the same size. They feel exactly the same. But in one important way, they are very different.

When I put this piece of material into this bowl of water, the water remains clear, and the color in the material remains the same. But when I put this piece of material into this bowl of water, it immediately begins to fade. See how discolored the water is already? The longer I leave the cloth in the water, the more the color will fade.

How many of you have heard someone called a "true friend"? What does being a true friend mean? Yes, a true friend is someone who remains your loyal and dear friend no matter what happens.

How many of you have heard someone called a "fair weather friend"? What does being a fair weather friend mean? Yes, a fair weather friend is someone who is your friend only as long as you can do something for him or give him something.

A true friend is steadfast and unchanging. He's like this piece of material whose colors have remained the same. But a false friend or a fair weather friend is like this other piece of material. The color is fading from the cloth and soon it will look faded and dingy. A false or fair weather

20

friend is true until he is put to the test. Then, like this material, he proves he is false.

When I put this piece of material into the bowl, the water was clear. Now see how discolored it is. The water is no longer clear. It is no longer useful. That is the way a false friend spoils a friendship. Loyalty keeps a friendship clear and clean over a long period, just as this piece of cloth made of true colors will keep this water, no matter how long it remains in the bowl.

—*Idalee Vonk*

Bearing Good Fruit

If a man remains in me and I in him, he will bear much fruit; apart from me you can do nothing. —*John 15:5*

Object Needed: A bowl of fruit

When we think of fruit, we think of a tree, for most of the fruit we eat grows on trees. In order to have good fruit we must have a good tree. The tree must be strong. It must be healthy. It must have a sturdy trunk securely planted in the ground so that strong winds will not uproot it. The ground in which the tree is planted must be good ground.

Next, in order to have good fruit we must take care of the tree. We must fertilize the ground around the tree so that the roots will have nourishment. Then we must prune the tree at the right time, cutting away any dead branches and clipping off parts of some branches so the tree will be well balanced.

Then, after the fruit forms we must spray the tree in order to keep insects from spoiling the fruit. So when we enjoy eating an apple or an orange or a tangerine or a pear

21

or a grapefruit we are enjoying the fruits of the labor of many people.

When the apostle Paul speaks of the "fruit of the Spirit," he is comparing us to fruit trees and the things we say and do to the fruit of the trees. Paul tells us the fruit of the Spirit is love, joy, peace, patience, kindness, goodness, faithfulness, gentleness, and self-control. How much of this fruit of the Spirit we have in our lives depends upon how much we love God and how firmly we believe in His Word.

We have said a tree must be firmly planted in good soil or a strong wind could uproot the tree and blow it over. Our lives must be firmly rooted in our love for God and our desire to live according to His Word, or strong winds such as hate, envy, stubbornness, and selfishness will uproot us and keep us from bearing good fruit. Next we must prune ourselves in order to bear good fruit, just as we have to prune the fruit tree by cutting away dead branches. The dead branches of our lives are bad habits, unkind words, and unkind acts.

Paul tells us if we keep ourselves strong and healthy by loving God with all our hearts and doing what we know is right, then we shall bear good fruit. Our lives will be filled with love, joy, peace, gentleness and faith. Everyone will love us because we love and help everyone around us.

—Idalee Vonk

Doing Our Part

"Well done, good and faithful servant! You have been faithful with a few things; I will put you in charge of many things. Come and share your master's happiness!"
— *Matthew 25:21*

Objects Needed: A blooming potted plant; a flower pot full of hard, dry soil

Some time ago a seed was planted in each of these flower pots. They started out the same—both were good seeds from the same flower. The person who planted the seed in this pot (the one without the plant) immediately forgot about it. He did not water the seed. He did not place the flower pot in the sunlight. So now he has nothing but a pot of hard, dry soil. But the person who planted the seed in this flower pot (the blooming plant) cared for it every day. He watered it and placed it in the sunlight. He cared for the young plant that grew out of the seed. Now he has a beautiful flower to enjoy.

God gives all of us talents, abilities, opportunities. The person who says, "God will take care of me"—and expects God to give him all he needs while he just sits back and waits—is like the person who did not care for the seed that was given to him.

But when we say, "God will take care of me and give me all I need, if I do my part and try my best," then we are like the person who took good care of the seed given to him, from which this beautiful flower grew. God has given us hands with which to work. He has given us minds to use, eyes to see, and talents and abilities so that we can do certain things well. If we expect God to do everything for us while we do nothing for ourselves, we are proving ourselves unworthy of His great love.

— *Idalee Vonk*

How to Please God

"Why do you call me 'Lord, Lord,' and do not do what I say?"
—*Luke 6:46*

Object Needed: A tape recorder

How many of you think that this is a good tape recorder? It looks like a pretty good one. But how can we tell for sure that it's a good one? That's right, we can turn it on and see if it works. If it works all right, then it's a good tape recorder. So let's give it a try (turn it on 'record'). Who would like to say something into the microphone so we can try it out? (Have someone say a few words.) Good, now let's rewind it and see if it can play back what we just recorded. It would not be much good if it could not play back what it recorded (play back what was recorded). There, now that we have tested it out, I think we can say that this is a good tape recorder—not because it looks like a good one, but because it works well and does what it is supposed to do.

In a way, the same sort of thing applies when we are trying to decide whether we are really a Christian or not. How good we might look to others does not really matter. What does matter is how well we *work.*

A tape recorder is judged by how well it records and plays things back. If it does these things, then it is a good tape recorder. A Christian is judged by how well he hears and then *obeys* the commandments of Jesus. If we just hear them when we come to church and Sunday school, but then do not follow them during the week, we are like a tape recorder that records but is not able to play anything back. That kind of a tape recorder would not be good for much of anything.

If we truly want to be sure we are Christians, then we

must obey as well as hear. Then God will be pleased with us, and He will call us His good and faithful children.

—Duane Kellogg

Rewards From Jesus

Rejoice and be glad, because great is your reward in heaven.   *—Matthew 5:12*

Objects Needed: A piece of candy; a quarter hidden in a bag

How many of you have ever watched 'Let's Make a Deal' on TV? Well, I want a volunteer this morning who would like to make a deal with me (choose one child). I'm going to give you this piece of candy. You can keep it or trade it in for what I have in this bag. What do you want to do? (Whichever he or she decides to do, continue on.)

In a way, Jesus wants to make a deal with us. We can keep what we have and stay the way we are, or we can trade it all in for what He has to offer us. Many people are afraid to let go of what they have. But those who do trade it in, and decide to accept Jesus as their Lord and Savior, are never disappointed. No matter how good things may have been before, I have never met anyone or heard of anyone who has ever regretted the trade.

If we will surrender our lives totally to Him, Jesus will give us back so much more that we will never be sorry for having done so. I hope all of you will make a deal with Jesus and give Him all that you are and have, because He has some wonderful things in store for those who do so.

—Duane Kellogg

Joy

No one will take away your joy.
—*John 16:22*

Object Needed: A small music box

This box looks like an ordinary box until we open the lid. Then we find it plays a lovely melody. Other music boxes may sound something like it: they may even play the same tune. But each box has a certain sound all of its own. When we close the lid, the music stops. The box will remain silent until someone lifts the lid. Then a beautiful melody pours out of the box.

No matter how closely we examine the box we cannot see any actual signs of the music. The happy sound is closed up inside this box, waiting to be set free. When we lift the lid, everyone who is close enough to hear will enjoy the cheerful little melody.

We all are much like a music box. There is a happy song closed up inside each of us, waiting to be set free. Some people go through life like a music box that has never had its lid opened. That is, they never share a happy song with others. They are always gloomy or unhappy about something. Yet, like a music box, they have a joyous song hidden within, ready to cheer all who are close enough to hear.

There is only one way we can lift the lid and release the happy song that is inside us. That is to live close to Jesus. When we do this, we will want to share our joyous song more and more often. And we shall want to release these joyous songs by spreading as much cheer and happiness as we can to everyone we meet each day, no matter who they are or where we may be.

—*Idalee Vonk*

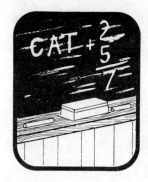

Repentance

Repentance and forgiveness of sins will be preached in his name to all nations.
—*Luke 24:47*

Objects Needed: Chalkboard, chalk, and eraser

(Write "Good Morning" on the chalkboard.) When we write something on the chalkboard and wish to remove it, we simply erase it (erase the writing). Now we can no longer see the words, "Good Morning," which were written on this board a minute ago and which we all could read. No matter how closely we look at this board, we still cannot see any trace of the letters. They have disappeared completely.

Sometimes when we write on a chalkboard we make a mistake (write "Good Mornimg"). We know better. We know that morning is spelled m-o-r-n-i-n-g, but we wrote an *m* instead of an *n*. As soon as the word is written, we realize we've made a mistake and immediately erase it. Then we write the word "Morning," spelling it correctly (do so).

It's very easy to make mistakes when we write on the chalkboard. It's also very easy for us to make mistakes when we are doing something at home or school, or even when we're playing. We know better, but somehow we make a mistake and say something or do something we know is not the right thing to say or do.

When we make a mistake while writing on the chalkboard, we can erase it and start all over. The old mistake is removed and we begin again with a clean slate. When we make a mistake in life, we can do the same thing through repentance. We must recognize our mistake. Then we must be sorry for what we have done and repent, that is, determine not to do that wrong thing again. Finally, we must remove the mistake or the wrong from our lives by

27

asking God to forgive us (and probably asking the person we have hurt, too). When God forgives us it is like erasing the mistake from our lives and giving us a clean slate to start all over again.

—Idalee Vonk

Reverence

God is spirit, and his worshipers must worship in spirit and in truth. *—John 4:24*

Objects Needed: A large flashlight or a desk lamp; an assortment of paper ranging from very thin transparent paper to thick dark paper.

Perhaps you never thought that there is more than one way to enter a church. But there are as many ways to enter a church as there are people entering it. This is what I mean.

Here we have a constant, steady light shining. When we hold this piece of cardboard in front of it, we completely hide the light. The cardboard is so thick that even though we are holding it close to the bulb, the light cannot pass through it.

Let's try these other pieces one by one. Each is thinner than the cardboard, but they are still too thick for the light to shine through. Now let's see what happens when we hold this piece of white typing paper before the bulb. It is thinner than the other pieces and we can begin to see the light. When we hold this piece of lightweight paper in front of the bulb, a little more light shines through. And finally, when we hold this very thin, transparent paper before the bulb, much light shines through.

This light is like the Spirit of God. It is always present. It is always brightly shining for us. These pieces of cardboard and paper are like people entering a church. Some people enter the church with minds so heavy and dark with personal thoughts that the light of God cannot shine through. They have not learned to put all worldly thoughts out of their minds when they enter the church. Therefore, their worldly thoughts become like this piece of stiff, black cardboard between them and the Spirit of God.

Some people go to church to please others. Some go because their friends go. Some people go to church, but do not enter into the worship service in any way. They sit in the pew and let their minds wander or think about things they are going to do during the coming week. Some people go to church and sleep through the service. Some whisper through the service. Some read. These people are all like the pieces of paper that are not so thick as the cardboard, but still keep out the light of God.

But when we go to church because we love God and wish to worship Him, and when we enter the church reverently and join in every part of the service, we find the Spirit of God waiting for us. We are like this thin, transparent paper. Our minds are so free from worldly thoughts and so ready for the Spirit of God that His light can easily enter our hearts.

—Idalee Vonk

It's What's Inside
that Counts

What goes into a man's mouth does not make him ''unclean;'' but what comes out of his mouth, that is what makes him ''unclean.''
—Matthew 15:11

Object Needed: An empty candy bar wrapper

How many of you would like to eat what I have brought with me here today? (Take the candy bar wrapper out of the bag; it should look like there is a candy bar inside.) Okay, here you go (give it to one of the older, more enthusiastic children, who will soon discover that it is empty). What's the matter? How come you're not eating what I gave you? It's just an empty wrapper, isn't it? That must have been disappointing—you thought you were going to get a candy bar and all you got was an empty wrapper.

When I held up this wrapper, you said you wanted to eat it because you thought there was a candy bar inside. You didn't want to eat the wrapper, did you? A candy bar wrapper is only important if it tell us what is really inside. If there is no candy bar inside, the wrapper is not much good for anything.

In a way, that's what it is like with us. God doesn't really care much what we look like on the outside—whether we're tall or short, fat or skinny, black or white or yellow. What we are like on the outside, how we look, even the things we do—these are only important if they show what we are like on the inside. As far as we're concerned when it comes to candy bars, and as far as God is concerned when it comes to us, it is what's on the inside that counts.

Only Jesus can fill us up inside with His goodness so we will not be like empty candy bar wrappers. I hope all of you have asked Jesus to become a part of your lives.

—Duane Kellogg

Courage

In this world you will have trouble. But take heart! I have overcome the world.
—John 16:33

Objects Needed: A lighted candle fastened in a candleholder; a jar; a piece of paper to be used as a fan

One of the first things we learn about fire is that it needs air in order to burn. If we were to put a jar over this lighted candle, the flame would go out because there would not be enough air to keep it burning.

But too much air blowing directly upon a candle will put out the flame. When I fan a distance away from the candle, it has no effect upon the flame. But the closer I stand to the candle while fanning, and the harder I fan, the more the flame flickers. If I stand close enough and fan hard enough, the flame will go out. The candle will not burn again until I hold a lighted match to its wick.

We are much like this candle. Our courage is like the flame. How brightly we shine depends upon how much courage we have. Troubles, difficulties, hardship, and handicaps are like the fan disturbing the air around the candle. When problems or troubles are small and far away from us, we can go right on burning brightly, for our courage is too strong for them to disturb or bother us. But the bigger the problems and the closer they come to us, the more courage it takes to keep smiling and be happy.

Once in a while a problem will come along that will seem too big for us, and we will feel we have not enough courage to go on. It's like the hard and close fanning that put out the candle's flame. We had to put a lighted match to the wick in order for the candle to burn brightly again. God is like the lighted match, for He alone can renew our courage and give us added strength to carry on in a useful way once again.

—Idalee Vonk

31

Commitment to Jesus

"Look how the whole world has gone after him!" —*John 12:19*

Object Needed: A picture of a TV or movie star the children would recognize

I brought a picture of someone with me today and I wonder if any of you can tell me who it is. (Let them tell you. It may be a good idea to have another one just in case they don't know the first). Have you ever met _____ (name of star) or talked to him? How did you know who this was? If you had a chance to ask him a question about himself, what would you ask?

We're all curious about famous people, just like the people who lived in Jesus' day were when they saw Him coming into Jerusalem on a donkey. They wanted to know who this man was and where He came from and what He was doing in Jerusalem.

Many people are still curious about Jesus today, and I'm glad all of you are curious enough about Him to come to Sunday school to learn more about Him. But remember, curiosity about Jesus is just the first step. It doesn't mean anything unless we take the second step of committing our lives to Him and being willing to obey Him. Jesus is more than just a superstar. He is the Savior and Lord of all who are willing to trust and follow Him.

—*Duane Kellogg*

Let Your Light Shine

Let your light shine before men, that they may see your good deeds and praise your Father in heaven.   —*Matthew 5:16*

Objects Needed: A light bulb that doesn't work, socket, cord, and plug

I brought a light bulb with me this morning for you to see. Light bulbs are amazing things, when you stop and think about it. We have them all over our houses and use them all the time, yet we hardly ever think about them.

Name some things you do at night in your home for which you use the light from a light bulb (let the children say things like read, sew, work on hobby, play games, see what's inside the refrigerator, etc.). That's right, a lot of things we do depends on the light from a light bulb like this one so we can see what we are doing (at this point, plug in the light bulb and turn it on).

Hey, this light bulb doesn't work. It's not coming on. What do you think I should do with it? (Let them make some suggestions and then continue.) If it doesn't work, it's not good for anything—so I may as well throw it out (place it in a waste basket).

You know, it's the same way with people who say they are Christians, but who don't *do* what Jesus tells them to do. They are like this light bulb that doesn't do what it is supposed to do.

It is important not only that we *believe* the right things, but that we *do* them as well. Sometimes this is a hard thing to do. Living a Christian life is not always easy. But if we do our best to live up to what we believe, we will find the price we have to pay is well worth it.

—*Duane Kellogg*

33

God Heals Us

... it was Jesus who had made him well.
—John 5:15

Object Needed: Some kind of medicine; for example, cough syrup

How are all of you feeling today? I brought some medicine with me this morning (show bottle). Can all of you see what it is? Do you know what it is for? That's right, it stops us from coughing. Have any of you ever taken cough medicine? Did it help?

Usually it does. But do any of you know what cough syrup is made of? Do you know what's in this medicine that makes us stop coughing? Well, do you have to know what's in it in order for it to work? It works just as well for us as it does for the doctors and scientists who know exactly what's in it and how it works.

Many people don't know what is *in* the cough syrup and how it works. Many people also don't know *who* makes it possible for those ingredients to do what they are supposed to do. Do any of you know who that is? That's right, it is God. If it were not for God and the way He makes the medicine work, we might never get well.

But even if we don't realize that it is God who actually heals us through medicines, God will still heal us. Just as we don't have to know what is in the medicine we take for it to work, so we don't have to know who makes it possible for it to work. How much better it is, though, to see and understand that only God can heal us, and that sometimes He uses medicines to help us get better. Then we will remember to thank Him when we are made well again.

I hope all of you will come to realize this and remember that only God can make you well.

—Duane Kellogg

What's Important?

If anyone gives a cup of cold water to one of these little ones because he is my disciple, I tell you the truth, he will certainly not lose his reward.
— *Matthew 10:42*

Objects Needed: Two simulated newspaper articles; one, a headline that reads "U.S. to send $100 Million in Aid to Korea," the other, a small article titled, "Family to House Missionary"

How many of you ever read the newspaper? Today I brought in two news articles that you might see in a newspaper. The first is one that you might see in big letters on the front page of a major newspaper like the *New York Times*. Will someone read out loud what it says? That's a lot of money, isn't it? Sounds like a pretty important piece of news.

The second is an item that might appear in a small local paper like the _____ (name of local paper). It's the kind of news item that might be in the second or third section of the paper. Let me read what it says, since it's probably too small for you to read (read title). Well, that's nice of that family to take in a missionary for a while.

Which of these two news items is really the most important? From our point of view, this first one, in the New York Times, is the most important because it involves so much money and probably a lot of people. But from God's point of view, this second article may be the most important. I say that because whenever we do something nice for one of Jesus' followers because he is a Christian, it's as if we do it for Jesus himself. That's the same as doing it for God.

The family who let the missionary stay in their home, eat their food, and use their utilities was actually sharing those things with God. And because they were willing to do those small things for the missionary, God is setting aside His

35

reward for them in Heaven. That will have eternal conse-
quences for them. The $100 million sent by the U.S. to
Korea wouldn't even last a year. Don't be fooled by something's bigness into thinking it is important. Small things
that we can do for each other may be even more important
than the things you read or hear about in the news.

—*Duane Kellogg*

Use Your Gift

We have different gifts, according to the
grace given us. If a man's gift is . . . serving, let
him serve; if it is teaching, let him teach.
—*Romans 12:6, 7*

Objects Needed: Screwdriver and pliers

I brought two things along with me this morning that I
want you to look at. Can all of you see what they are? Now
what can you do with a screwdriver? (Let them mention a
few things like tighten or loosen screws, take lids off paint
cans, etc.) A screwdriver can do quite a lot of things, can't
it?

Okay, what can you do with pliers? (tighten a nut, pull
teeth, grip things, etc.) Lots of things can be done with
pliers. But can I take out a screw with pliers? Can I tighten
a nut with a screwdriver? Does that mean the screwdriver
is better or more useful than the pliers? Or are the pliers
better or more useful than the screwdriver?

Each one of these tools was made to do a specific thing.
We don't use one to do the thing the other tool was made
for. Depending on what we're doing, we may use one tool a
lot more than the other one, but each tool is valuable for
what it is able to do.

You know, we are a lot like these tools. God made each
one of us to do a particular thing. He has given us certain

gifts and abilities to do what He wants us to do. Sometimes God will want to use us a lot more than someone else because of what He wants to get done. But just because God gives us a lot of work to do, it doesn't mean we are better than anyone else. Neither does it mean we should complain because we seem to be the only ones doing anything.

God wants us to do our jobs, whatever they may be, regardless of what He has other people do. God may want you to help out around the house or on the farm because He's given you the ability to do a good job. Don't worry about what your brothers and sisters and friends do—that's between them and God. If you just do what *you* are supposed to do, then God will be pleased with the way you obey Him.

—*Duane Kellogg*

Being a Peacemaker

Blessed are the peacemakers, for they will be called sons of God. —*Matthew 5:9*

Objects Needed: A hammer; a bowl or cup that is cracked or dispensible

Here is a bowl. As long as it is used for serving food, then carefully washed and dried and stacked away in the kitchen cabinet, it will go on being useful for a long time. But if someone came along with a hammer and hit the bowl like this, it would no longer be useful. (Break the bowl with the hammer, being careful so the chips do not fly.) Now, as you see, the bowl is nothing but a pile of broken pieces.

Peace is like this bowl before it was broken, when it was pleasant to look at, when it could have been used each day, when it served and helped people in many ways. This hammer is like jealousy, hatred, spite, greed—anything that destroys peace between us and others. Unkind words. Arguments. Unwillingness to do our share of the work at home or at school. Just as this hammer ruined this bowl, so these things I have just mentioned ruin peace among us and others.

I was wasteful. I broke a bowl that still could have been used. Destroyers of peace are always wasteful. Those things in our everyday lives that ruin peace are all wasteful. They cost friendships, they cost happiness, and they waste many precious hours.

We could glue this bowl together again, but it would take a long time to fit each piece in its proper place. It would take a great deal of patience to glue the pieces together so they would hold fast. But no matter how carefully the pieces were fitted and glued together, we always could see each place where the bowl was broken.

When two people quarrel, it takes much time, patience and understanding to patch their broken friendship. A patched friendship is never as beautiful as one that never has been ruined by a quarrel.

Jesus said, "Blessed are the peacemakers." Whenever we are tempted to quarrel with someone or to start a fight, we should try to remember these words and become the peacemaker instead of the fighter.

—*Idalee Vonk*

Living Up to Our Claims

Jesus said, "'If you were blind, you would not be guilty of sin; but now that you claim you can see, your guilt remains." —*John 9:41*

Object Needed: A product that does not live up to the commercial claims made about it

How many of you have ever bought something that sounded really good on TV, but after you bought it you found out it didn't live up to the claims made about it? How did you feel?

I brought some glue with me that I bought awhile ago. The package makes some pretty big claims about this glue. Let me read to you what it says (read or share some of the advertising claims made about the product). Sounds pretty good, doesn't it? Well, let me show you how well it worked on something I used it on (show pieces of a broken item on which the glue didn't work).

When something does not live up to the claims made about it, we get a little angry at the people who made the product, don't we? The same thing happens when Christians don't live up to the standards that they are supposed to. People watch us if we go to church and call ourselves Christians. If they see us doing wrong things and behaving like everyone else, it gives Jesus and His church a bad name. Then when we try to tell them about Jesus and what he has done for us, they won't listen. Our actions speak louder than our words.

So if you want to tell others about Jesus, you must remember to try your best always to live up to the standards that Christians are supposed to go by. Otherwise, no one will listen to you and Jesus will be given a bad name. Think of yourself as a walking, talking, living advertisement for Jesus, and maybe that will help you live the way you know you should.

—*Duane Kellogg*

A Real Christian

[Jesus] replied, ''My mother and brothers are those who hear God's word and put it into practice.''   —*Luke 8:21*

Object Needed: An artificial plant in a pot (try to make it look as real as possible)

How many of you like to plant things and watch them grow? Many people seem to enjoy taking care of plants. Can any of you tell me what kind of plant I have here in this pot? (Let the children guess) Let me tell you. It's an artificial plant made out of plastic. It's meant to look real, but it really isn't. It's just an imitation of the real thing. Putting it in a pot with dirt around it makes it seem even more real. But putting an artificial plant in a pot does not make it real. Putting someone in church or Sunday school doesn't makes him a real Christian, either.

What do we have to do to become real Christians? Let me tell you. First, we have to repent of our sins, which means telling God we are sorry we have disobeyed Him. Then we have to ask Jesus to come into our lives and fill us with His Spirit, and be baptized in His name. That makes us come to life; some people call it being born again. Finally, after we have done that, then we must follow Jesus and worship Him by coming to church and doing what He wants us to do during the week.

I hope all of you are real Christians, and not just artificial ones. And if you are, I hope you will always remember to take time out to worship God and to tell your friends at school how wonderful Jesus has been to you.

—*Duane Kellogg*

Be Faithful to the End

But the Lord is faithful, and he will strengthen and protect you from the evil one. — *2 Thessalonians 3:3*

Object Needed: An engagement ring

Can anyone tell me what this is? (Hold up the ring and let them guess.) That's right, it's an engagement ring. A man often gives a ring like this to the woman he is planning to marry. Have any of you ever given or received an engagement ring? No? That's because none of you plan on getting married right away, correct?

When you become a Christian, though, and accept Jesus as your Savior and Lord, it's like becoming engaged to Him. He promises to never leave us, and we promise to follow Him wherever He calls us to go. We also promise to obey Him and to remain faithful only to Him.

Just like engaged people are not supposed to date anyone else, we as Christians are not supposed to turn away from Jesus and follow the ways of those around us. It shouldn't make any difference to us if "everyone else is doing it." If Jesus doesn't want us to do it, then that's all we should need to know.

We must remain faithful to Jesus all the time, because someday He is going to come for us and take us to be with Him forever. We want to be ready when He comes; we don't want to be found doing things that displease Him. We should always be faithful to Jesus and do what He wants us to do.

—*Duane Kellogg*

41

God Draws Us Closer

"Will not God bring about justice for his chosen ones, who cry out to him day and night? Will he keep putting them off?"
—Luke 18:7

Object Needed: A long string with a prize tied to one end of it

I need a volunteer this morning whose parents will let him or her have _____ (whatever the prize is). As you can see, I have a prize here that I want you to have. But first let me put it on the floor and I'll go back here (unwind the string while talking and backing up) and wait. All right, go ahead and pick up the prize (when the child reaches for it, pull it part way toward you; continue doing so until the child is right next to you and then hand him a duplicate prize that has not been on the floor). There is your prize. Thank you for your help this morning.

Now some of you may be wondering why I kept pulling the prize away from _____ (name of child) until he was right up next to me. I did it to teach a very important lesson about how God sometimes acts toward us. Sometimes we want or need something very badly, and we pray that God will give it to us. Only He doesn't seem to do what we ask. We wait and wait and nothing seems to happen.

What God is often trying to do by making us wait is to draw us closer to himself. By drawing what we want away from us, like I did with _____ (child's name), it makes us come closer and closer to Him. And if it is something God wants us to have, and we keep asking for it and seeking after it, then sooner or later we not only will get what we wanted, but we will also be drawn closer to God.

Try to remember that the next time you think God is ignoring your prayers. He isn't. He's just trying to draw you closer to himself.

—Duane Kellogg

God's Laws

Object Needed: A prize hidden somewhere in the church building

I need a volunteer who can follow directions well (select an older child). Okay, now I want you to do just what I say. First of all, stand up (then give a number of directions, like *walk straight ahead, turn right*, etc., until you have directed the child to where you have hidden his prize). Because you have obeyed everything I said to you, you have come to the place where you can now receive your reward. I want you to reach out your hand and take the prize I have hidden (wherever it is). Very good, you may go sit down.

One of the reasons it is very important for us to obey Jesus is so that we can receive the blessings He wants to give to us. As we obey Him, we come to the place where He can give us many good things. Just like when (child's name) obeyed me, he came to where I had a reward waiting for him.

So don't forget, the rules and commandments we have in the Bible are not there to make our lives more difficult. They are there so that we can follow them and thus be in a better position to receive the blessings of the Lord.

—*Duane Kellogg*

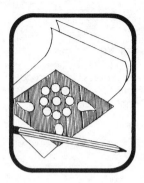

Jesus, Our Perfect Example

I have set you an example that you should do as I have done for you.　　*—John 13:15*

Objects Needed: A pencil, paper, and a cutout pattern of something (flower, bird, etc.)

When we want to draw a dog and want it to look as much like a dog as possible, we find a pattern of a dog and trace around it. We do not use just any old pattern; we choose the very best one we can find—the one that looks exactly like a dog in every way.

Then we place the pattern on our piece of paper and draw around it, following the shape as carefully as we can. If we're not careful or if the pencil slips, we won't have a very good picture of a dog. But if we are careful and follow the pattern exactly, we will draw a fine picture of a dog (demonstrate with the pattern, drawing the figure as you speak).

The first important thing we had to do was find the best pattern of a dog that we could find. Then we had to be very careful to follow the exact lines of the pattern in order to draw the best picture we could.

If we want to live the best life possible, we must first choose the best pattern we can find. The best pattern we can possibly find for our lives is Jesus. If we try very hard to talk like Jesus would talk, act like Jesus would act, think like Jesus would think and do the things Jesus would do if He lived on earth today, then we are following our pattern very closely. When we follow the pattern of a dog very closely, we are able to draw a fine picture of a dog. When we follow the pattern of Jesus very closely, we are able to live a fine Christian life.

—Idalee Vonk

Helping Each Other

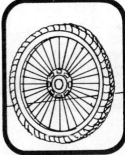

"Love the Lord your God with all your heart and with all your soul and with all your mind." This is the first and greatest commandment. And the second is like it: "Love your neighbor as yourself." —*Matthew 22:37-39*

Object Needed: A wheel with spokes, hub, and rim, large enough to be seen by all the children

As you see, this wheel has many spokes. They are all held together by the hub, which forms the center of the wheel. There is a definite place for each spoke in the hub. Sometimes these spokes get broken or become loose and come out. When that happens, the whole wheel becomes weaker because of the missing spoke. No other spoke can take its place or do its work.

The opposite end of each spoke has a definite place in the rim. When a spoke is missing, there is a vacant place in the rim, and the space between the rim and the hub is made weaker because of the missing spoke.

The world in which we live is like the rim of this wheel. God's love is like the hub. And we are like the spokes. The only way God's love can live on this earth is through us, for part of us is connected to God in Heaven and part of us is connected to the earth in which we live.

The best way we can show God's love is by helping others. Jesus taught us to love each other—that means to help each other. When we fail to do this, we are like broken spokes in a wheel. We no longer connect God's love with the earth. Just as no other spoke can do the work of the broken one, no one else can do our work. When we fail to help others, we not only break the connection between God's love and the world, but (like the broken spoke) the kingdom of God is made weaker because we have failed to do our part to keep it strong. —*Idalee Vonk*

Spreading Happiness

And now these three remain: faith, hope, and love. But the greatest of these is love.
—1 Corinthians 13:13

Object Needed: A shallow basin of water and some pebbles

Let's see what happens when we drop one of these small pebbles into this basin of water. As you see, circles form around the place where the pebble fell into the water. The circles continue to spread and become wider and wider. This happens every time we throw a pebble into the water.

Now if we had a pool of water in our backyard and we threw larger stones into it, the circles would be larger and spread over a wider area.

When we love others we want to help them. We want to do kind things for them. We want to make them happy. Doing a kindness for someone because we love him or her is just like throwing a pebble into the water. Just like the pebble started circles to form on the water, so the love we show for a friend starts circles of love to form. The friend we made happy with our love will want to make someone else happy the same way. Others will see how much happiness our loving kindness is creating. They, too, will want to make someone else happy.

The larger the stone we throw into a bigger pool of water, the larger will be our circles. The more love we show, the more happiness we spread and the greater the circles of love we form. Sometimes the love for others that one person has in his heart starts a circle of love so big it reaches around the whole world.

—Idalee Vonk

46

Selfishness

Freely you have received; freely give.
—*Matthew 10:8*

Objects Needed: A knife; a paper bag; two apples, a delicious-looking one and a rotten one

This morning I'm going to tell you a story about two boys who both received an apple and what each boy did with his apple. Listen carefully! I'm going to ask you a question when I finish telling the story.

John and Larry helped Mr. Wilson clean his basement one Saturday afternoon. In addition to a shiny quarter, Mr. Wilson gave each of them a beautiful luscious-looking red apple when all the work was done.

On the way home, Larry thought, "I don't feel like eating an apple right now. But if I take it home, Mary will see it. Then I'll have to share it with her. I know what I'll do! I'll hide the apple inside my jacket. When I get to my room I'll put it in a paper bag and hide it in my closet. Then I'll eat it later when I'm all alone."

So Larry put his beautiful red apple in the paper bag and hid it far back on the top shelf of his closet (hold up the bag with the rotten apple inside).

On the way home John looked at his apple. It was so red and so beautiful and looked so delicious. He opened his mouth to take a big bite. But then he thought, "No. I won't eat it now. This is the nicest apple I've seen in a long time. I'll take it home and give Mom half."

As soon as John arrived home he cut the apple in half (cut the apple in half. Later, cut the apple into fourths as you speak). Just as John was giving his mother half of the apple, Jane and her friend, Barbara, came home from skating.

47

"Oh, what a beautiful apple!" Jane cried. "Are there more?"

"No, Jane," mother replied. "Mr. Wilson gave this one to John, and he gave half to me. You may have half of my piece."

"And you can have half of mine, Barbara," John said.

So both John and his mother cut their half of the apple in half once again. Now there were four pieces, one for each of them.

Larry's apple lay hidden in the paper bag on the top shelf of his closet for some time, because he had forgotten all about it. Weeks later when he remembered the apple he hurried to his room, took the brown bag down from the shelf, put his hand inside and what do you think he pulled out? A rotten apple (go through the appropriate motions as you speak).

Now my question is, "How many people did John's apple make happy, and how many people did Larry's apple make happy?"

What do you think the two boys learned from what happened to their apples?

—*Idalee Vonk*